Defender of the Rain Forest

CHICO MENDES

by Joann J. Burch

A Gateway Green Biography
The Millbrook Press
Brookfield, Connecticut

To Ann, Davida, Joan, and Karen,
with many thanks for being
such a supportive writing group

Published by The Millbrook Press
2 Old New Milford Road, Brookfield, Conn. 06804

Library of Congress Cataloging-in-Publication Data
Burch, Joann Johansen.
Chico Mendes, defender of the rain forest / by
Joann J. Burch.
p.   cm.—(A Gateway green biography)
Includes bibliographical references and index.
Summary: Discusses the life and work of the Brazil-
ian rubber tapper whose efforts to secure fair treat-
ment for other tappers and to preserve the Amazon
rain forests resulted in his murder in 1988.
ISBN 1-56294-413-4
1. Mendes, Chico, d. 1988—Juvenile literature.   2.
Conservationists—Brazil—Biography—Juvenile literature.   3. Rubber tappers—Brazil—Biography—
Juvenile literature.   4. Rain forest conservation—
Amazon River Region—Juvenile literature.   5. Deforestation—Control—Amazon River Region—Juvenile literature. [1. Mendes, Chico, d. 1988.   2.
Conservationists.   3. Rubber tappers.   4. Rain forest conservation—Amazon River Region.] I. Ti-
tle.   II. Series.
SD411.52.M46B87   1994
333.75'06'0981092—dc20   [B]   93-1198   CIP   AC

Cover photo courtesy of Paulo Jares/Abril Imagens
Photos courtesy of Imagens Da Terra/Impact Visu-
als: pp. 4 (Ricardo Funari), 8 (top: Julio Etchart), 15
(Kit Miller), 22 (Ricardo Funari), 27 (top: Julio Etchart, bottom: Milton Guran), 30 (top: Jesus Carlos), 35
(top: Ricardo Funari), 42 (Ricardo Funari); Photo Re-
searchers: pp. 8 (bottom left: Kenneth W. Fink, bottom right: Jeanne White), 11 (bottom: Claudia
Andujar); Miriam Romais: p. 11 (top); Abril Imagens:
pp. 18 (Paulo Jares), 30 (bottom), 40 (André Penner),
43 (Paulo Jares); Sipa Press: p. 35 (bottom).

Chico Mendes

Over 3,000 kinds of trees grow in Brazil's rain forest.
Widespread cutting has threatened many. In this photo,
a worker with a chain saw prepares to bring down a tree.

Chico Mendes heard the buzz of the chain saws. Then the sounds of branches snapping and vines popping filled the air. The ground shook as a giant tree came crashing down. Frightened birds scattered. Screeching monkeys scrambled into hiding.

Trouble had come to the Amazon rain forest of Brazil, in South America. Ranchers were clearing the forest to make room for their cattle to graze. Cutting crews were ripping out acres of trees hundreds of years old. The rain forest was Chico's home, and it was being destroyed.

Chico organized peaceful protests to stop the cutting. When he learned that any part of the forest was going to be cleared, he rounded up all the men, women, and children he could find. They marched through the forest until they came to where the trees were being cut.

Then the protesters linked arms and formed a human wall between the trees and the workers with the chain saws. None of the protesters carried weapons of any kind, which was very scary when they faced eight-foot-long chain saw blades. Chico walked up and down the line of protesters, calming them in his quiet way. The workers didn't want to hurt anyone, and they usually laid down their saws.

The ranchers who hired the chain saw crews also hired gunmen to shoot anyone who tried to stop the cutting. But when the gunmen saw women, children, and unarmed men, they put down their weapons. Then the workers and the gunmen walked away.

The ranchers and other people who thought they could make money by cutting down the rain forest grew very angry with Chico for this. They threatened to kill him if he didn't stop making trouble. But Chico devoted his life to defending the rain forest. Here is his story.

Chico Mendes lived in the largest tropical rain forest left on earth. It covers much of northern Brazil. The Amazon River, one of the world's largest and longest rivers, runs for four thousand miles through this area. So does the equator. The climate is hot and humid year-round. There are only two seasons, rainy and dry. But even during the "dry" season, rain falls nearly every afternoon.

The Amazon rain forest is the sort of place where more kinds of plants and animals grow than almost anyplace on earth. Ninety types of frogs and toads can be found in a few square miles. Fifty-four kinds of ants make their home in the area. There are more varieties of fish in the Amazon's waters than in the entire Atlantic Ocean.

Some of these plants and animals grow very big. Picture a tree as high as a twenty-story building. Brazil nut trees often get to be this tall. Think of a spider big enough to eat a small bird. Some spiders in the rain forest grow this large. Imagine a bright-blue butterfly with wings as big as a grown-up's hand. Morpho butterflies sail through the forest on wings eight inches wide.

Chico Mendes was born in the rain forest on December 15, 1944. His full first name was Francisco, but almost everyone called him by a shortened version of that name, Chico. He lived in the state of Acre (pronounced AH-cray), in northwestern Brazil. This region is part of Amazonia, the forested land surrounding the Amazon River.

Chico was the oldest child in his family. His parents had seventeen children, but only six sur-

Above: The Amazon River is longer than the U.S. highway that stretches between New York and San Francisco. In this photo, it winds through miles of rain forest. Right: Among the many beautiful and unusual animals that live in the Amazon rain forest are this toucan and this tapir.

vived into adulthood. There were no hospitals or doctors in the rain forest. If a sick person couldn't be cured with plants from the forest, he or she died.

The Mendes home was a typical rain forest house. It was very small and was built on thick stilts about three feet high. Building the house off the ground kept out crawling insects and wild animals. The stilts also kept the house from being flooded during rainstorms.

In front of the house was a veranda, or porch. Inside were small bedrooms. At the back, the kitchen jutted out on a platform. The floorboards of this platform were spaced slightly apart so that crumbs and dishwater could fall to the ground below. The family's pigs, chickens, and ducks gobbled up the crumbs and grains of rice.

Chico's grandfather and father were rubber tappers. They collected latex from a type of tree in the forest called *seringueira* (pronounced sair-een-GAIR-ah). This is also known as a rubber tree. Latex is a milky sap that flows out from under the bark of such trees. When latex is heated and put through a process called curing, the sap thickens, darkens, and becomes rubber.

When Chico was nine years old, he learned how to tap rubber trees. It wasn't an easy job. He and his father left home before dawn, after eating a breakfast of thick coffee and manioc porridge (a kind of tropical oatmeal). Each day they tapped 150 to 200 rubber trees along one of three trails that looped around their house.

When they came to a rubber tree, Chico's father carefully cut a **V** into the tree's soft bark with a special knife. Chico used a small branch to prop a tin cup or the empty shell of a Brazil nut at the bottom of the **V**. The milky sap leaked from the cut into the cup or shell.

Chico and his father moved quickly from one tree to the next. The trees were dozens of yards apart. Each trail was eight to eleven miles long. While they hiked along the trails, they kept their eyes and ears open for animals they could shoot for meat. Sometimes they killed an armadillo, a porcupine rat, or a monkey. Tapir, ancient cousins of the horse, and deer were special prizes but rarely seen.

By mid-morning the trail led them back to their

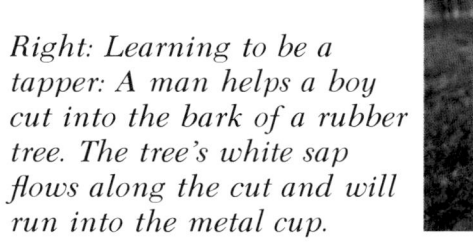

Above: This photo shows a rain forest house on the Amazon River. Like Chico's, this house is built on stilts to avoid flooding.

Right: Learning to be a tapper: A man helps a boy cut into the bark of a rubber tree. The tree's white sap flows along the cut and will run into the metal cup.

house. They were hungry by then and ate a hearty lunch of beans, rice, and manioc biscuits. If hunting had been good that week, they also had a little meat.

After lunch, Chico and his father retraced their steps along the same trail they had hiked that morning. They collected the latex that had flowed into the tin cups and shells. After pouring the sap into a rubber-coated sack or a metal jar, Chico hung the cups and shells on a stick beside the trail.

By the end of the day they returned home with several gallons of raw latex. Even though they had walked sixteen miles or more, their work was not finished. They still had to cure the latex. Chico's father built a fire, and Chico threw palm nuts into the flames to make the fire smoky. Smoke prevents the growth of mold or fungi in the latex so that it can become good-quality rubber.

Only when the latex was cured did the Mendes family eat dinner. Afterward, Chico always asked his father to give him a reading lesson. As they sat on the veranda night after night, Chico learned to read by the smoky glow of an oil lantern.

By the time he was eleven years old, Chico was reading letters and old newspapers aloud to the other tappers. Everyone admired how such a young boy could read so well. Most tappers never learned to read, write, or do math because there were no schools in the rain forest. The rubber bosses wanted it that way. The bosses bought the tappers' rubber. Very often they cheated the tappers without their knowing.

But Chico's father knew, and it made him angry. When he put his rubber on the bosses' scales, they said it weighed less than it really did. If he told them they had made a mistake, the bosses said they didn't make mistakes. They said they were simply subtracting for water or insects trapped in the rubber.

Chico's father and the other tappers in the area did business with the rubber bosses in a town called Xapuri (pronounced sha-poo-REE). Here the bosses also ran the only stores in the region where tappers could buy food and supplies. When the bosses didn't pay them in full for the amount of rubber they brought in, the tappers bought what they needed on credit and ended up owing money.

Chico saw how the tappers were being kept in debt to their bosses. When he grew up, he worked hard to change this system.

Chico learned a lot in town, but he had many teachers. The rain forest itself was a school. During his early morning hikes along the shady rubber trails, Chico saw colorful birds called toucans feasting on palm nuts. When he turned over a log, thousands of beetles scurried away. He found cacao beans, used to make chocolate, sprouting from the trunks of certain trees. Everything seemed to have its place in the forest.

Chico also learned to recognize plants and other things that could be used to heal sick people. Termite nests built on the sides of tree trunks could be ground up and boiled for a tea to cure bad coughs. The root of a bamboo stem could be soaked in water and used to reduce swelling. Today, people all over the world use drugs made from rain forest plants.

Although he didn't know the word, Chico was learning about ecology. Ecology is the study of how

A tapper family waits while a merchant weighs a ball of their rubber. To them, the difference of a few pounds could mean making enough money to eat or not—just as it did for Chico's family.

living things relate to their environment and to each other. The people of the forest lived in balance with their environment. They set a good example of how to live in the forest without destroying it.

Tappers took care not to cut too deeply into the rubber trees. Deep cuts damage trees, and they can die. Trees that had been tapped were left to rest for a few days before any new cuts were made. This allowed them to live long, healthy lives. Some rubber trees in the rain forest are two hundred years old.

By the time Chico was eleven years old, he was as good a rubber tapper as any adult. He felt that he was part of the forest. As he made his way along the trails, he talked to the rubber trees. He jingled their cups to ask if they were going to give him lots of latex. The trees seemed to answer him by shaking their leaves.

Chico was planning to be a rubber tapper for the rest of his life. However, one day when he was twelve years old, he met a man who would change his life forever. According to one account, Chico and his father were at home curing rubber when the man emerged from the forest and approached their house. The man was dressed like a tapper—in shorts, T-shirt, and flip-flop sandals. But he didn't speak like one. Chico had never heard anyone talk so well, and he was fascinated by the words the man used.

The man was Euclides Tavora, and he carried newspapers with him that told what was happening in the world. Chico's father had always bragged about how well his son could read. But Chico realized there were many words in Tavora's newspapers that he had never heard before.

Even so, Tavora noticed how intelligent Chico was. He invited Chico to his house to take more reading lessons. Because the house was a three-hour walk away, Chico's father agreed to let his son spend the weekends with Tavora and his books and newspapers.

For the next three years, Chico and Tavora read newspapers every weekend and discussed government and politics far into the night. Tavora was a well-educated man and taught Chico how to

Another account of how Chico met Euclides Tavora
says that they first saw each other in a rubber boss's
store in Xapuri. The city is shown in this photo.

read better and how to write and think more clearly.

Chico stopped going to Tavora's house when Chico's mother died after giving birth to her seventeenth child. Chico and his brother Raimundo took over the tapping full-time. Their father stayed home to care for the younger children and tend the crops. One day Raimundo tripped in the forest and his shotgun went off, killing him. Then Chico took his next oldest brother, nine-year-old Zusa, into the forest to teach him how to tap rubber trees.

Since Chico didn't have time to visit Tavora, Tavora came to Chico. On Saturday nights they went to a rubber boss's meeting place. The boss had a radio, a luxury in the rain forest. They listened to news broadcasts of stations from all over the world, such as Voice of America, the British Broadcasting Corporation, and Radio Moscow. Then they discussed the different versions of what was happening in the world and tried to arrive at the truth.

When Chico was twenty years old, Tavora became ill and went to the state capital for treatment. He never returned. Chico said, "Without him I was half lost. But I started to teach other rubber tappers how to read and write. They all wanted to learn, because when you could read you saw how much the store was cheating when it bought your rubber and sold you food."

Chico wrote hundreds of letters to important people in Brazil's government describing how the rubber tappers suffered. They were forbidden to have schools, he explained, so that the rubber bosses could cheat them without anyone knowing. There were no hospitals, and many people died when they got sick, including Chico's mother.

Every week Chico wrote at least one letter, but he received only a few useless replies. He soon realized that the government was not going to help the rubber tappers. They would have to help themselves. He would show them how.

He remembered what Tavora had taught him. The only way the tappers could improve their lives was by working together for change. Chico tried to talk them into forming groups to stand up for their rights. The tappers weren't interested. They had worked alone all their lives and didn't think they could change anything by uniting.

When he was twenty-five years old, Chico married his neighbor's sixteen-year-old daughter, Eunice Feltosa. The marriage lasted only two years because he spent most of his time away from home. When he wasn't tapping rubber, he was trying to unite the rubber tappers. In 1971 Eunice took their baby daughter and returned to her family.

That year marked an important change in Chico's life. He quit tapping rubber full-time and began teaching adults to read in a small government school just outside Xapuri. He wasn't paid, so he tapped trees for other rubber tappers to earn a little money. He also continued talking to tappers about uniting against the rubber bosses.

One of the tappers he worked for had three daughters. Chico taught them to read. He gave them their first lesson of the day before he left on his morning's circle of the rubber trail. After he returned, he gave them their second lesson. One of the girls, ten-year-old Ilzamar Gadelha Bezerra, idolized Chico. She cried when he took a job in Xapuri. She never forgot what a difference learning to read made in her life. Chico never forgot her

Chico Mendes also helped educate children in the rain forest. He got the government to put up schools for the children of tappers, like those attending class in this rain forest school.

either. When she was twenty years old, he married her.

Shortly before Tavora had left for the state capital, he had given Chico a radio. From listening to the radio, Chico learned that the Brazilian government was planning to open Amazonia to settlers. Amazonia made up more than half of Brazil's territory and was the only place in the country with land to spare.

At that time, 30 million people lived in slums surrounding Brazil's big cities. Many were farmers with no land and no skills for city life. Crowded into slums, these people were causing big problems. The government wanted to send them to Amazonia. They used the slogan: "Land without people for people without land."

Anyone willing to move to the rain forest was promised enough money for a two-room house and a plot of land. In addition, the government promised to provide schools, medical clinics, and a general store.

Thousands of people flocked to the rain forest. They cut and burned the trees on their plots of land. Then they planted crops. But the soil was so poor that after two or three plantings, nothing would grow.

The settlers abandoned the ruined plots of land and moved to other parts of the rain forest. This meant cutting down more trees. After a few plantings, the same thing happened as before. Many people became so discouraged that they moved to towns along the rivers. Since there were no jobs, they ended up living in new slums.

Meanwhile, parts of the rain forest where Chico and the other tappers lived and worked had been destroyed forever. With no trees to provide shade, the barren soil was baked by the tropical sun and washed away by heavy rains.

In addition to small plots for farmers, the Brazilian government offered large areas of rain forest land to ranchers. The idea was for ranchers to raise cattle and sell beef to countries such as Japan and the United States. This would bring much-needed money into Brazil.

The ranchers damaged the rain forest far more than the farmers did. Cattle need a lot of land to graze on. Ranchers cut down thousands of trees to make enough room for them. The chain saws and bulldozers the ranchers used destroyed much of the rain forest.

The governor of the state of Acre, where Chico lived, welcomed ranchers. Acre was the poorest state in Brazil. Only a few places had electricity, and television didn't arrive until 1974. The governor thought ranching would help his state and bring in a lot of money.

The fact that Indians and rubber tappers like Chico were already living on land the ranchers wanted didn't matter. The Brazilian government had advertised land, and the ranchers were going to take it, regardless of who was living there. As they saw it, the Indians did not count and the tappers would simply have to make way for progress.

The Indians retreated deeper into the forest or moved onto land set aside for them called reserves. Thousands of tapper families moved across the border to the country of Bolivia. Others went to the state capital, where most ended up living in slums.

This angered Chico. He told the tappers they had the right to stay on the land they had worked for years. He said if they would unite, they could fight this new threat to their homes and livelihood.

But the tappers still weren't ready to fight for their rights.

Other people tried to help the rubber tappers as well. One man, Wilson Pinheiro, came from southern Brazil to try to get unions started in Amazonia. He taught classes in land rights and union organization in a town thirty-five miles from Xapuri. When Chico heard about this, he moved to a nearby farm. He and Pinheiro became close friends and helped form the first chapter of the Rural Workers Union in Acre in 1975. Chico was elected secretary-general of the union.

In 1977 Chico moved back to Xapuri. A rubber merchant invited him to run for a seat on the town council and paid for his campaign. Chico won the election. As a councilman, he spoke out about the rights of tappers. Tappers soon looked up to him as their leader.

By this time the ranchers were becoming violent in their attempts to take land that they wanted. They burned the tappers' houses and turned cattle loose on their crops to trample and

Above: Cattle graze on rain forest land that was deforested—cleared—until only few trees were left. Right: Deforestation affected more than trees. It threatened the traditional way of life of rain forest Indians. This photo shows a young Kayapó Indian in traditional dress and with tatoos.

eat them. They also hired gunmen to frighten the tappers. Sometimes tapper families were rounded up and loaded onto a boat. The gunmen would take them downstream and say, "We are going downriver. When you see a beach you like, we'll drop you there. That will be your new land."

When other rubber tappers learned what the ranchers were doing to their fellow tappers, they were finally ready to fight for their rights. Hundreds joined the chapter of the Rural Workers Union that Chico set up in Xapuri in 1977.

The Catholic Church gave the union a small shed for its headquarters. The Church also provided space for training sessions and discussion groups to figure out how to stop the ranchers.

The best idea turned out to be the *empate* (pronounced em-PAH-tay). An *empate* is a blockade formed by people standing in front of the trees they want to save. In the United States it would be called a demonstration.

Not every *empate* was successful, however. Sometimes the tappers marched for miles through the forest only to find the chain saw crews had already cut the trees. Other times, ranchers hired military police or gunmen to turn the demonstrators away.

But tappers kept up the pressure against cutting down the forest. The *empates* that succeeded in blocking the cutting crews made ranchers very angry. They decided to teach the leaders of the *empates* a lesson. In 1979 four men wearing masks dragged Chico into a car as he walked through town. They drove out of town, beat him badly, and dumped him on a dirt road.

Chico was lucky they only beat him. Several priests and lawyers who had helped the tappers were shot and killed. In 1980 Wilson Pinheiro was killed, gunned down on the porch of the union hall.

The success of Chico's peaceful *empates* made him many enemies. The government and the ranchers accused him of being against progress. Chico replied he wasn't against progress. He was against destruction of the rain forest and of the rubber tappers' way of life.

Chico's union continued to add new members. Soon it became strong enough to fulfill one of Chico's dreams. For the first time, schools were set up in the rain forest and tappers' children could

Right: The Rural Workers Union headquarters. The banner on the wall reads: "Basta," which means "No More." Below: Chico speaking to rubber tappers of the importance of preserving their rain forest home.

learn to read and write. But the destruction of the rain forest continued.

In the late 1970s, newspapers around the world began to publish articles about the Amazon rain forest. Environmentalists came to Amazonia to see for themselves what was happening. (An environmentalist works to protect the balance of plants and animals in nature.) They learned of the efforts of Chico Mendes to save the rain forest.

Chico was pleased to hear how people around the world had become aware of problems in the rain forest. In 1985 he helped organize a meeting of rubber tappers to discuss these problems. Held in Brasilia, the capital of Brazil, the meeting brought together more than 120 men from all over Amazonia.

During the meetings the rubber tappers talked about how to stop the ranchers from cutting down and burning the forest. Chico told them the government had passed laws to protect the lands, or reserves, where Indians lived. Why couldn't the same be done for the rubber tappers? Chico proposed they ask the government to set aside areas where tappers could harvest latex. These could be called "extractive reserves" because tappers "extract," or take out, latex from rubber trees.

The Brazilian government agreed to set up a few extractive reserves for rubber tappers because this would help preserve some of the Amazon rain forest. But the government's main interest was still in turning Amazonia into farms and ranchland.

When Chico returned from the meeting in Brasilia, he hiked the rubber trails again to tell everyone about extractive reserves. He also began to talk about ecology.

The ranchers didn't care about ecology. They were only interested in cutting down the forest to make pastures for their ranches. So Chico organized more *empates* to stop the cutting. Some ranchers tried to bribe Chico into calling off the *empates*. They offered him cattle and money, but Chico refused. This angered them even more.

He may have angered the ranchers, but he became a hero to environmentalists. In 1987 Chico was invited to Miami, Florida, and Washington, D.C., to talk about the destruction of the Amazon rain forest. He spoke before the U.S. Congress and various environmental groups. He explained how the rubber tappers and Indians lived without hurting the trees or harming the land. He said he wished his government would do more to prevent the ranchers from destroying the land.

When Chico returned home, his airplane flew over the Amazon rain forest. He was shocked to see how bad things really were. Dozens of fires burned where ranchers were clearing the land. The smoke was so thick in some places that he could not even see the tops of the trees.

Others were looking down at the fires as well. Scientists using space satellites to observe the rain forest estimated that 170,000 fires had burned in Amazonia in 1987. The smoke from all those fires was polluting the air, not just over Brazil but also in other parts of the world.

Fires give off carbon dioxide, a gas that traps much of the sun's heat near the earth's surface. If too much carbon dioxide is released, our planet warms up. Scientists call this the greenhouse effect. Moreover, trees are major absorbers of carbon dioxide. When they are cut down, there are fewer trees left to absorb the gas. As a result, more carbon dioxide remains in the atmosphere.

If the earth's temperature rises too much, resulting in global warming, the large masses of ice at the northern- and southernmost parts of the planet might melt. With all that extra water released into the oceans, there could be flooding all over the world. Therefore, it is important to preserve the earth's trees so they can absorb carbon dioxide.

In 1987 Chico won two important awards in recognition of the work he had done to save the Amazon rain forest. The United Nations Environmental Program honored him in London, England, with its Global 500 Award, given to world leaders in conservation and environmental action. The Better World Society awarded him its Protection of the Environment Medal.

Chico *had become* an internationally honored environmentalist. But when he returned to Brazil, the government and many people were angry. They thought Chico was giving the world the im-

Above: Looking down on wasted land: Fires burn miles of the rain forest land in this photo, while smoke pollutes the atmosphere.

Right: The internationally honored environmentalist takes a moment's break with his wife Ilzamar and their son Sandino.

pression that Brazil was anti-environment. One man on the Xapuri town council made fun of Chico's awards. "That was not a medal," he said. "That was a rattle to put on a donkey's neck."

Ranchers were still cutting down trees, and Chico resumed his *empates.* The blockades were so successful that in 1988 they saved more than 20,000 acres from destruction. Ranchers were very angry with Chico and the other union leaders.

The Alves da Silva family were particularly upset. They had recently bought land for a ranch in Acre. When Chico heard they were getting ready to cut down their trees, he persuaded several hundred people to gather for an *empate.* They marched through the forest to where the family lived. They stayed on the outskirts of the ranch until the Alveses gave up the idea of cutting down the forest.

The protesters slept in nearby homes and in the schoolhouse. Chico brought in supplies such as milk, butter, meat, and eggs in the union's pickup truck. His aunt cooked big pots of rice and beans for the protesters. Finally, the Alves family realized the tappers were not going away, and they sent away their chain saw crews.

The family had a bad reputation. They had fled to Acre to escape being imprisoned for crimes they committed in another part of Brazil. When Chico learned that Darly, the father, and his brother Alvarino were wanted for murder, he told the police. Before going into hiding, Darly went around Xapuri telling people, "I'm going to get that troublemaker Mendes."

On May 24, 1988, Chico received a death threat. Someone called him on a neighbor's telephone and said he would not live out the year. Chico moved his wife and two young children into town where he rented a small house. He asked the governor for protection. Two military policemen were assigned to be with him at all times.

Tappers told Chico they had heard that the ranchers had a meeting to discuss getting rid of him. Chico sent letters to everyone from the governor of Acre to the president of Brazil listing the people who were planning to kill him. No one answered the letters.

At least six attempts were made on his life. Although he became increasingly nervous, he continued doing union business surrounded by bodyguards with machine guns. When people asked him why he didn't move away, Chico said he didn't want to be a coward.

On December 22, 1988, after being gone for a few days on union business, he came home for the Christmas holidays. He played dominoes with his two bodyguards until his wife told him to clear the table so they could have dinner. It was hot and muggy, and Chico decided to take a quick shower before dinner. He threw a towel over his shoulder and opened the door to the backyard, where the shower was.

Darci Alves da Silva, Darly's son, and several other gunmen were hiding in the thick brush outside. When they saw Chico open the door Darci shot him. He staggered back inside the house and collapsed on the floor. As soon as the bodyguards heard the shot, they ran for their lives. Ilzamar rushed to her husband's side, but it was too late. Chico Mendes was dead.

She ran into the street screaming, "They've killed Chico." But the policemen sitting outside the sheriff's office on the next corner did not get up. They were friends of the Alveses.

Word of Chico's murder spread quickly. Rubber tappers hiked for many hours through the forest to attend his funeral. More than a thousand people attended his funeral on Christmas Day. People from the forest as well as friends from the world outside Amazonia paid their respects. As they walked by his casket, they talked about how Chico Mendes had changed their lives and made the world a better place.

His death made front-page headlines in New York and London. Usually when someone was deliberately killed in Amazonia, the murderers were never caught. Because of the worldwide attention, however, the Brazilian government was forced to investigate Chico's murder. Roadblocks were set up, house-to-house searches were made, and 150 police officers swept the forests.

The prime suspects were the Alveses. Darly Alves da Silva, and his son Darci finally came out of hiding and surrendered. Darly's other son, Oloci, was captured in a shootout. After two years of delays, they were brought to trial in Xapuri's small wooden courthouse. Darly was found guilty of planning Chico's murder. Darci was convicted of

Although they mourned his death, thousands at Chico Mendes's funeral kept alive the spirit of his empates, or protests. People in this photo carry a banner that reads, "They killed our leader but not our struggle."

firing the shotgun that killed him. Each received a nineteen-year prison sentence. In 1992, however, Darly was released from prison.

The death of Chico Mendes brought worldwide support to his movement to save the rain forest. In 1989 several United States senators flew to Acre to talk with the governor and tapper leaders about environmental programs. (The group included Senator Albert Gore, Jr., who later became the vice president of the United States.) Brazil passed new environmental laws, and forest police began patrolling the forest to stop illegal cutting and burning.

The Brazilian government approved a plan to replant 2.5 million acres of deforested areas of the Amazon rain forest. The president of Brazil promised to create more extractive reserves and national parks throughout Amazonia. The first to be established was the 2.4-million-acre Chico Mendes Extractive Reserve. Today three thousand families gather rubber and Brazil nuts without fear that ranchers will cut and burn the forest around them.

At the opening of the U.N. Conference on Environment and Development, hundreds of children gather to sing. They are showing support for the fight to save natural resources like the rain forest. It is a fight that Chico Mendes lived and died for.

In 1992 leaders from all over the world met in Brazil for the United Nations Conference on Environment and Development. The conference helped focus the world's attention on the destruction of our earth's environment. It was fitting that it was held in the country that had been the home of Chico Mendes, who lived and died a defender of the rain forest.

A plaque at Chico Mendes's grave.

Important Dates

1944 Born on December 15 in Acre, Brazil.

1956 Meets Euclides Tavora.

1969 Marries Eunice Feltosa. Marriage ends in 1971.

1971 Moves out of the forest and into Xapuri; becomes a union organizer.

1977 Begins organizing *empates*. Wins a seat on Xapuri town council; speaks out for tappers' rights.

1983 Marries Ilzamar Gadelha Bezerra.

1985 Proposes "extractive reserves" as an alternative to ranches at a meeting of rubber tappers in Brasilia.

1987 Flies to United States to speak to environmentalists about the Amazon rain forest and becomes an internationally acclaimed ecologist. Receives United Nations' Global 500 Award and Better World Society's Protection of the Environment Medal.

1988 Organizes *empate* against the Alves da Silva family ranch. Murdered by Darci Alves on December 22.

Further Reading

About Chico Mendes

DeStefano, Susan. *Chico Mendes: Fight for the Forest.* New York: Twenty-First Century, 1991.

About Rain Forests

Baker, Lucy. *Life in the Rainforests.* New York: Franklin Watts, 1990.

Banks, Martin. *Conserving Rain Forests.* Austin, Tex.: Steck Vaughn Library, 1990.

Bender, Evelyn. *Brazil.* New York: Chelsea House Publishers, 1990.

Hoff, Mary, and Rodgers, Mary M. *Our Endangered Planet: Tropical Rain Forests.* Minneapolis: Lerner Publications, 1991.

Landau, Elaine. *Tropical Rainforests Around the World.* New York: Franklin Watts, 1991.

Rowland-Entwistle, Theodore. *Jungles and Rain Forests.* Morristown, N.J.: Silver Burdett Press, 1987.

Wonders of the Jungle. Washington, D.C.: National Wildlife Federation, 1986.

Index

About the Author

Joann J. Burch became interested in the Chico Mendes story after a stay in the Amazon rain forest of eastern Peru, not far from western Brazil where Mendes lived. This is her fourth biography for young readers. She has also published numerous travel articles about her adventures throughout the world. Her passion is travel, and her hobbies include photography, tennis, and collecting figurines. She lives in Beverly Hills, California, with her husband and three college-age children.